Super Crazy Fun

BIG KID PHONICS

2
Short Vowel Sounds

WARNING!

Lots of crazy words!

i

Author: Matthew Hitch

Co-author: Sunok Moon

Illustrator: Matthew Hitch

Cover Design: Brittany Hitch

Layout Design: Matthew Hitch

Text Design: Matthew Hitch

Image Manager: Matthew Hitch

~~Vain Meglomaniac: Matthew Hitch~~

Credits Editor: Matthew Hitch

Image Manager Manager: S.Moon

Image Manager Manager Control: Absolutely no one

Artistic Arguer: Sunok Moon

Dishwasher: Matthew Hitch (occasionally Sunok Moon)

Title: Captain Matt's Super Crazy Fun

Big Kid Phonics 2 Student Book

ISBN 979-11-93590-26-3

First published 2023

Published by Hitch Publishing

info@supercrazyfun.net

This textbook came about as the result of 20 years of trying to make kids enjoy learning English. It is designed around the use of the rhotic R and other characteristics of English pronunciation common in North America. We believe it can be used in other parts of the world as most phonics books can, and we are keen to hear feedback from anyone who tries this.

We want to make clear that the word "crazy" used in the title is in relation to any of the common definitions illustrated below, and does not refer in any way to the meaning "insane."

strange/illogical   **wild**   **unexpected**   **fun**   **unwise**

About the Authors:

Matthew Hitch has taught English in Korea for the better part of 20 years and holds a master's degree in applied linguistics. He clearly does not have a pig nose, and by most accounts is not at all malodorous. He also cuts a dashing figure according to his wife.

Sunok Moon prefers to go by the name Michelle, and is in fact quite scary as reported in the bio on the back of this book. She has a degree in English literature and has taught English in Korea for approximately 3 weeks longer than Matthew, who is writing this and finds it weird to refer to himself in the third person.

Contents

Welcome parents and teachers!

Thank you for considering our book. Phonics books are notoriously boring, so this is the last bastion of publishing where even the tiniest bit of creativity can raise the bar (sorry phonics book publishers, but it's true). With that said, we humbly offer you our content. We have also intentionally challenged convention in a few ways. Much of what we have to say may be used or discarded though, and these books can be used just like any other mainstream phonics book. We hope you will choose to use whatever you please and dispose of the rest.

Please allow us to explain just where our method of teaching phonics may diverge from mainstream approaches, and please do forgive us for sharing information from what is undeniably the most mind-numbingly boring and seemingly useless field of study, linguistics. Most phonics books are not written by scholars in the field of linguistics. They are mostly written by early childhood educators, so perhaps that's the first divergence. We'll start with how we sound out consonants. In linguistic studies it is not uncommon for consonants to be distinguished by using a vowel (usually "ah") on both sides. This means a "V" sounds like "ahvah" and an "F" sounds like "ahfah" and so on. Most phonics books distinguish consonant sounds without such preceding vowel, but they do follow with a vowel in the form of the schwa. This is fine for most consonants, but the ones that are able to be maintained until breath is exhausted can be confusing with a schwa where they end a word. It's mostly ESL students who feel this confusion, but we think it doesn't hurt to teach those consonants without a schwa to native speakers as well, so where "V" sounds like "və" in most phonics books, in our book it is presented as "vvvvvvv" with no schwa. We apply this to all long consonant sounds in our audio files (L,M,N&R are also presented as long with a tiny schwa sound at the end though). If you have read this far, we take our hats off to you. Most would be fast asleep by now.

The next divergence is our use of Magic E. We chose Magic E for the fun potential. The Split Digraphs just can't seem to hold a crowd. Magic E is no longer used in most educational settings for many reasons, but mostly because as a rule it cannot be defined clearly. We do mention that split digraphs are better though, mainly to extend an olive branch to all the teachers we hope will buy our books.

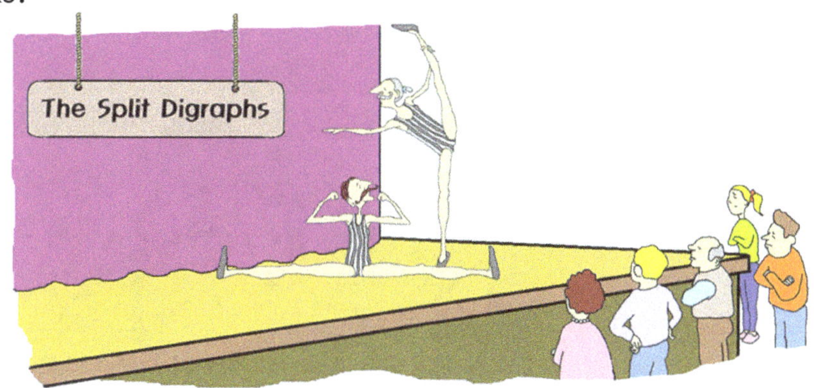

And the final divergence we would like to mention is our choice of words. Our choice of words may seem a bit odd at times throughout the books, but we chose them for their potential for keeping kids engaged over their usefulness. We approach a phonics book as a tool to teach about sounds much more than vocabulary. Poop, vomit, spit, fart, snot, and burp are the most popular with our students. We tried to find a spot for booger, but alas...

Our word choice is also strange in that it includes words that have the long E vowel when teaching split digraphs. Most phonics books glance over the long E vowel. The argument we have heard for this is that it is difficult for the younger students, but we suspect that it's avoided more because it's difficult for authors to find suitable words. We decided to give it a try, and our experience is that the long E words we chose are not that difficult for our students to grasp. Given that English is their second language, we believe native English speaking kids will cope with them just fine. Also you may notice our sight words are not all actually sight words - oops! Anyway, we hope you enjoy our silly books.

Welcome students!

Okay, so now let's learn
how to put sounds together.

Tracks 0-9

We write them close together,
so we say them close together!

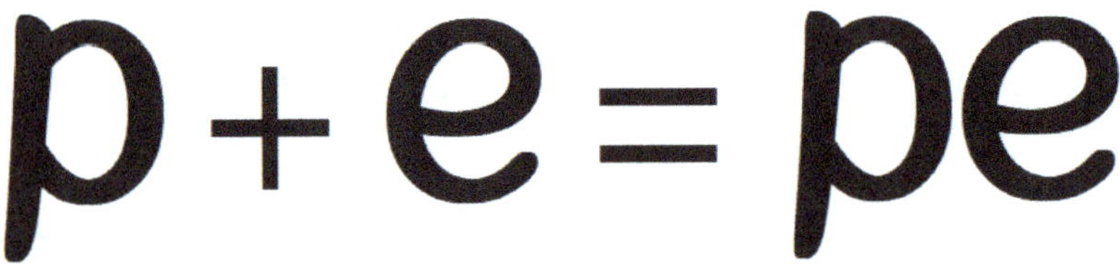

$$p + e = pe$$

But we don't just write them close together like a bunch of grapes!

They all have to be in a straight line!

Let's get started...

Sounds

Vowels

Tracks 0-9

Name	short sound	
A	a	
E	e	
I	i	
O	o	
U	u	

"Sometimes Sounds"

**Many letters have "sometimes sounds."
Sometimes A makes the same sound as
the letter U! You can hear it in the
word"banana." We use the sometimes
sound for the word "a."**

**O and U have the same
"sometimes sound."**

Strange isn't it?

Practice with your teacher:

1.	2.	3.	4.
	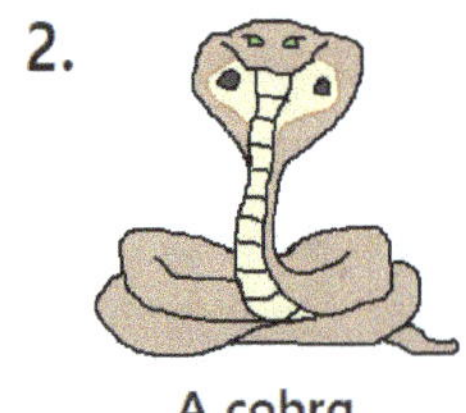		
A banana	A cobra	A panda	A puma

Consonants

Tracks 0-9

Some consonants change when we put them into words.
The long-sounding consonants usually don't change.

a   +   m   =   am

Track 7

But most short-sounding consonants change a lot.
At the end of a word we only use half the sound.

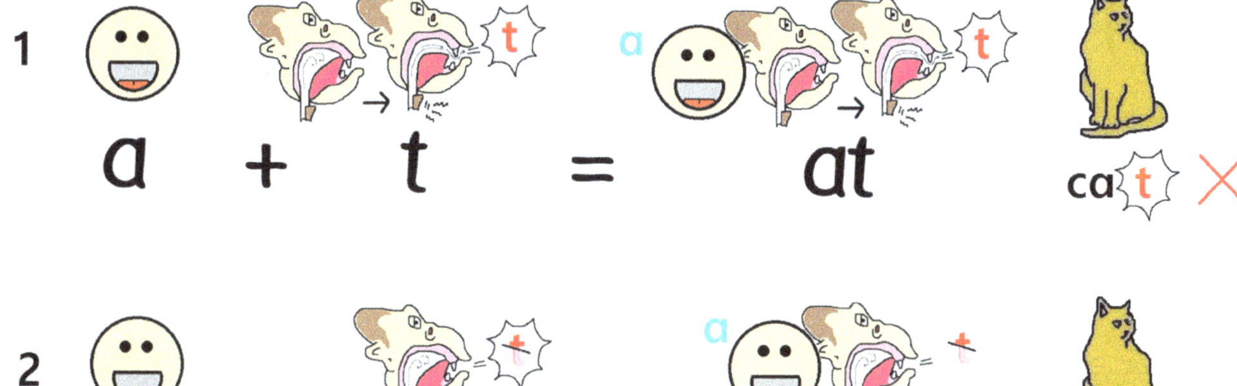

1   a   +   t   =   at   ca**t** ✗

2   a   +   t   =   at   ca**t** ✓

Track 8

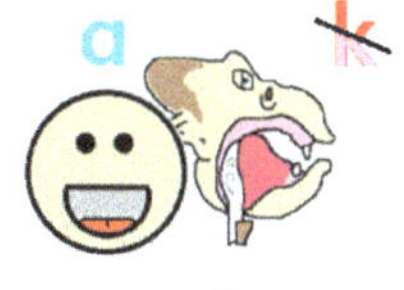 1. ak
 2. ag
 3. ap
 4. ab
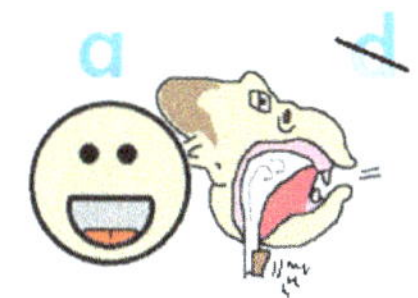 5. ad

Listen, point, and make the sound:   Track 9   Words with **a** 

Tracks 0-9

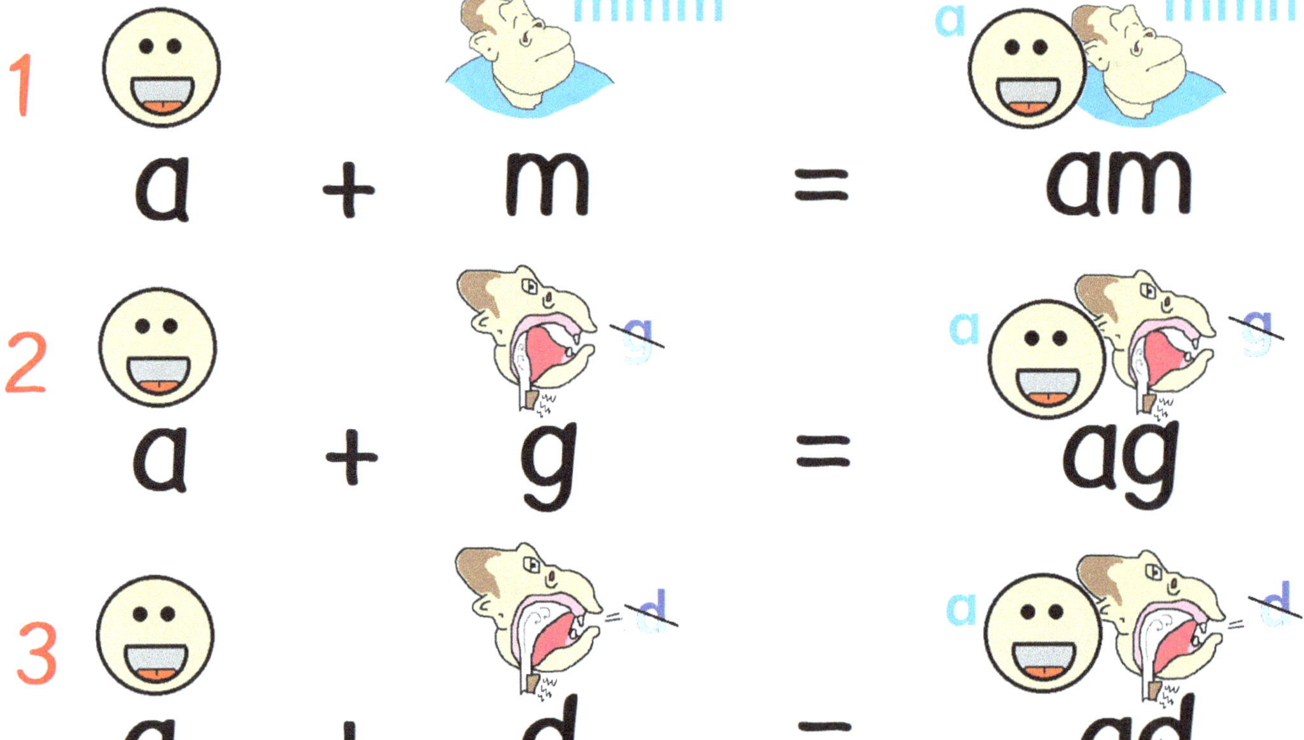

Listen, point, and say the word: Track 10

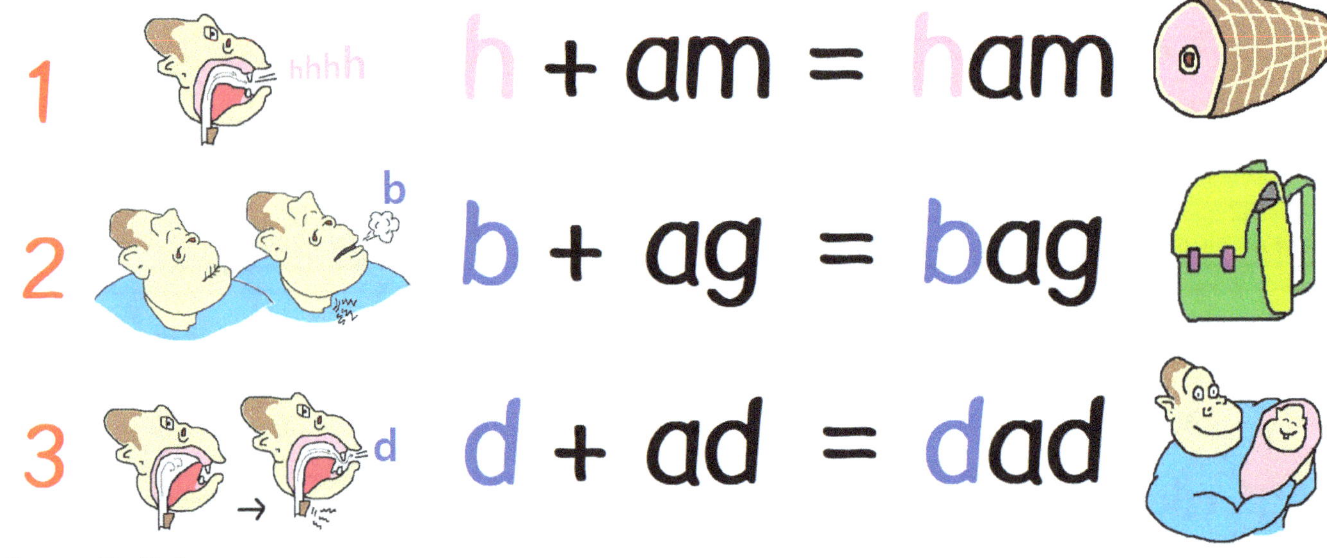

Follow the rules

1 h + am = __________ 

2 b + ag = __________ 

3 d + ad = __________ 

4 m + an = __________ 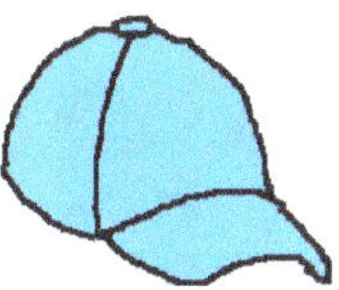

5 c + ap = __________

6 f + at = __________ 

New Words

Listen, point and repeat the new words

ad

bad   **dad**

ag

bag   **nag**

am

ham   **jam**

an

fan   **man**

ap

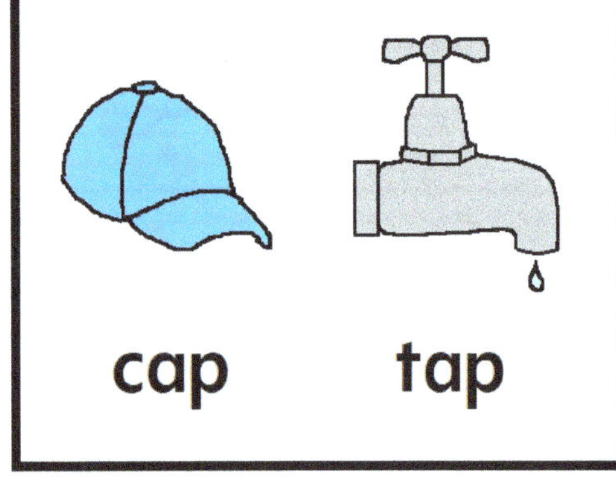

cap   **tap**

at

fat   **rat**

Exercises

Listen and write the last two letters

Tracks 10-19

1 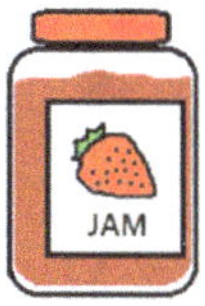   j _______

2 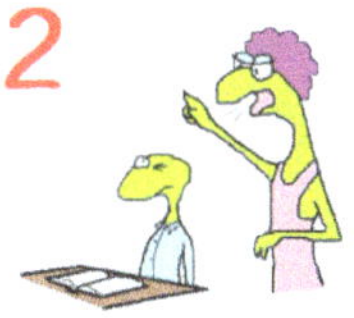   n _______

3 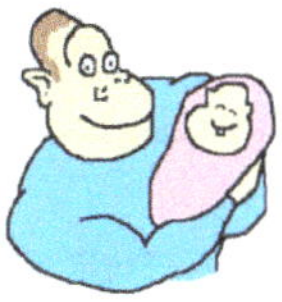   d _______

4 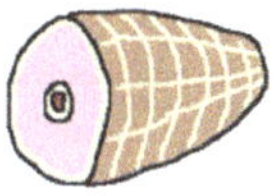   h _______

5 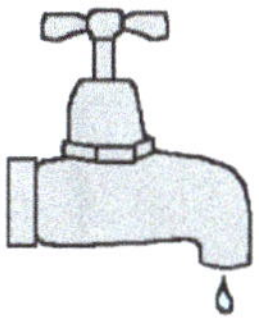   t _______

6 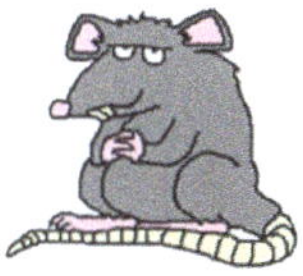   r _______

7 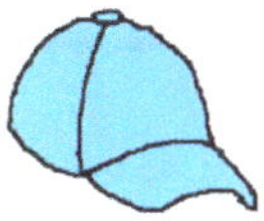   c _______

8 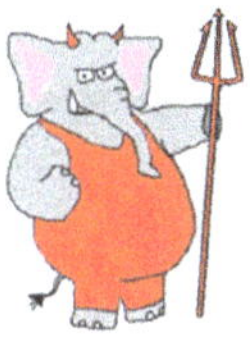   b _______

9 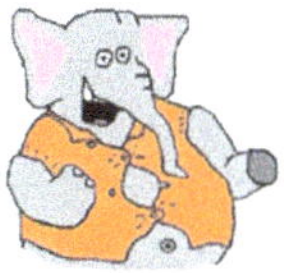   f _______

10 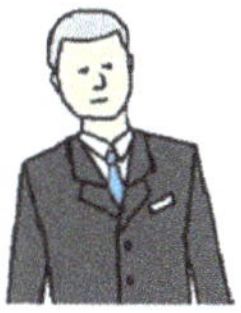   m _______

Listen and circle the right letters AND picture

1 am ap ad 

2 am ag an 

3 ap ag ad 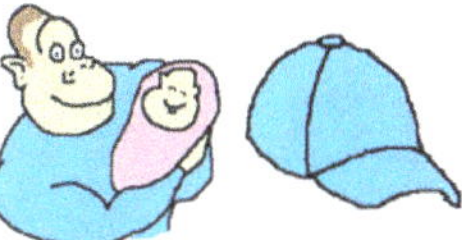

4 an at ap 

5 ap ag at 

6 am ag ad 

Exercises

Circle the word you hear

Tracks 10-19

Write the word to match the picture

Chant

Nag the man,
nag the man,
nag the bad man.

Turn off the tap!
Turn off the fan!

Nag the man,
nag the man,
nag the bad man.

Story

Track 16

Tracks 10-19

1. am   ag   ad   2. am   ap   at

3. an   at   ad   4. am   ag   an

5. ap   ag   at   6. ap   ag   ad

Listen and read along    Track 17   Sight words: have   that   yummy   what

Listen, point, and make the sound:  Track 18 Words with e 

Tracks 10-19

1  e + 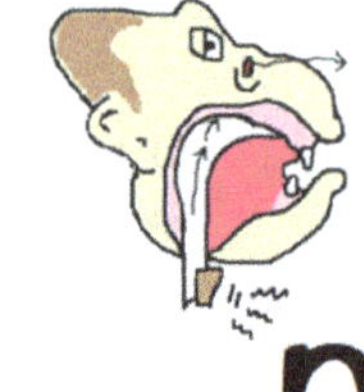 n =  en

2 e + d = ed
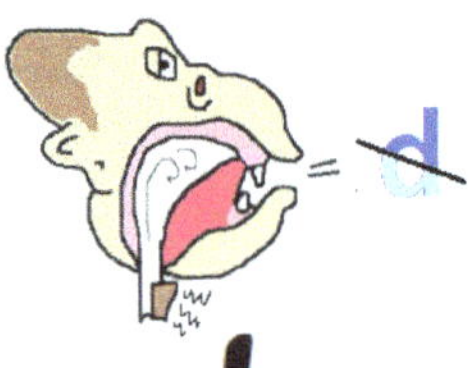 

3 e + g = eg
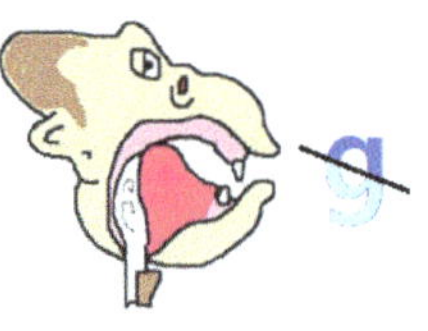 

Listen, point, and say the word:  Track 19

1  m + en = men 

2 r + ed = red 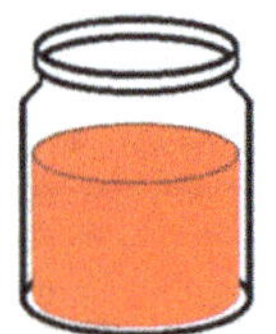

3 l + eg = leg 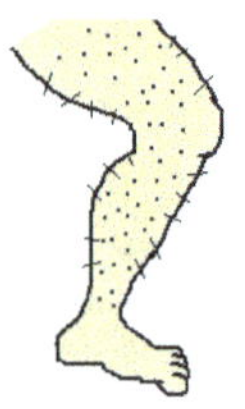

Follow the rules

Write the words

1 m + en = _________

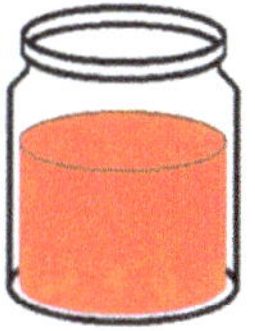

2 r + ed = _________

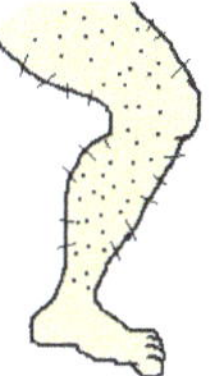

3 l + eg = _________

4 w + et = _________

5 b + ell = _________

6 D + eb = _________

New Words

Tracks 20-29

eb 

Deb   web

ed 

red   wed

eg 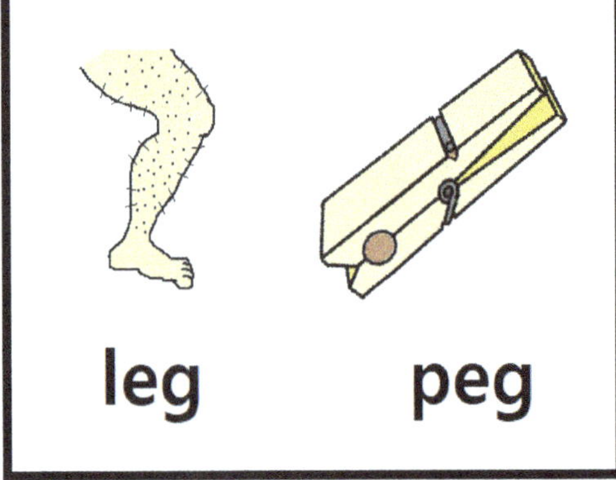

leg   peg

ell 

bell   well

en 

men   pen

et 

pet   wet

Exercises

Tracks 20-29

Listen and write the last two letters

1 p _______

2 p _______

3 w _______

4 w _______

5 l _______

6 r _______

7 w _______

8 b _______

9 w _______

10 m _______

Listen and circle the right letters AND picture

1 en ell eg 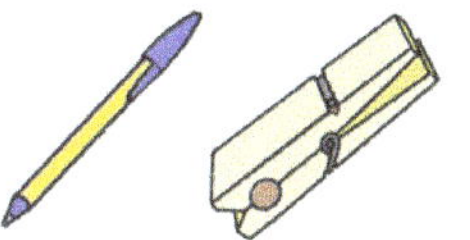

2 et ed eb 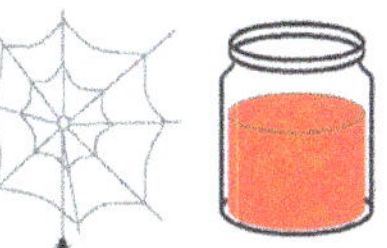

3 en ell ed 

4 et eb eg 

5 eg en ed 

6 ell et eb 

Exercises

Circle the word you hear

Tracks 20-29

Write the word to match the picture

Chant

New sight words: she wear so scary will

Peg Leg Deb,
She wears red,
She's so scary,
Peg Leg Deb.

Peg Leg Deb,
I will wed,
She's not scary,
Peg Leg Deb.

18   Unit 2

Story

Circle the last two letters of the word you hear

Track 25

Tracks 20-29

1. ed eb eg
2. ed eb ell

3. en ell et
4. et en ell

5. eg en et
6. ed eb eg

Listen and read along

Track 26

Sight words: fell down am / are

Listen, point, and make the sound:   Track 27 Words with **i** 

Tracks 20-29

1 i + n = in

2 i + p = ip

3 i + g = ig

Listen, point, and say the word: Track 28

1 b + in = bin 

2 r + ip = rip 

3 w + ig = wig

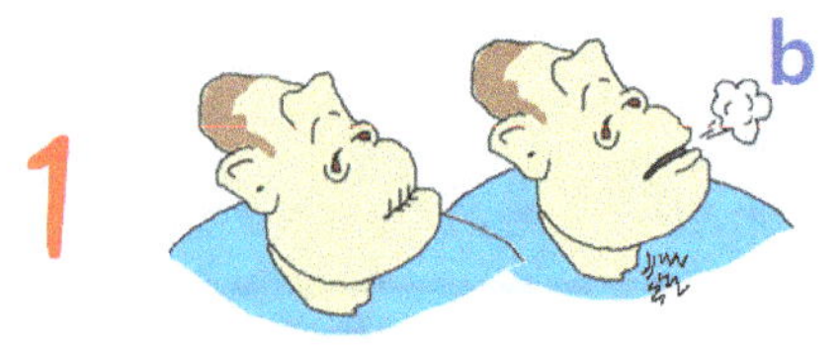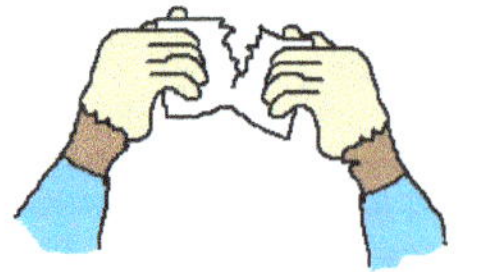

Follow the rules

1 b + in = _______ 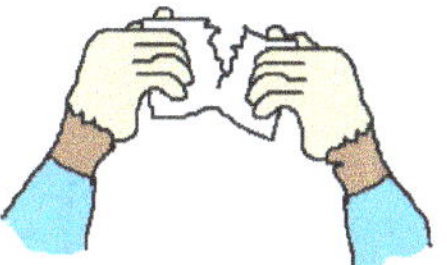

2 r + ip = _______

3 w + ig = _______ 

4 s + it = _______ 

5 r + ib = _______ 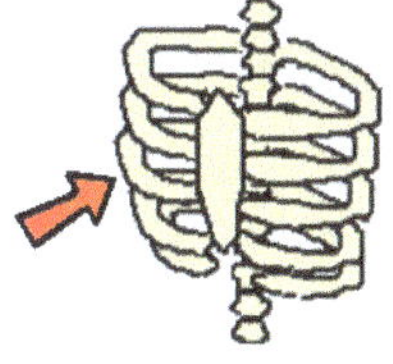

6 k + id = _______ 

New Words

Listen, point and repeat the new words

Track 29

ib

bib   rib

id

kid   lid

ig

big   wig

in

bin   fin

ip

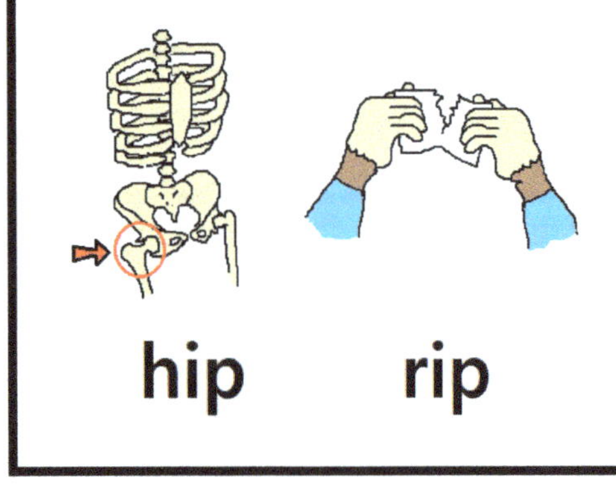

hip   rip

it

hit   sit

Exercises

Listen and write the last two letters

1 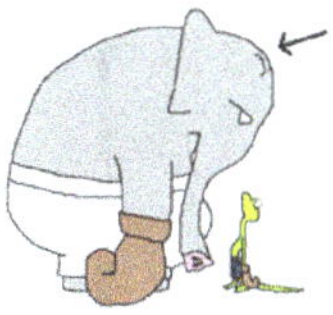   b ______

2 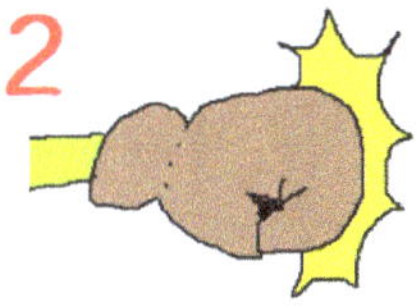   h ______

3 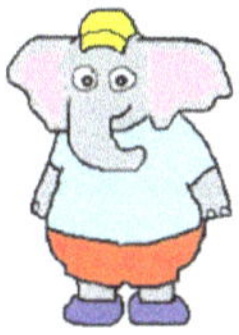   k ______

4 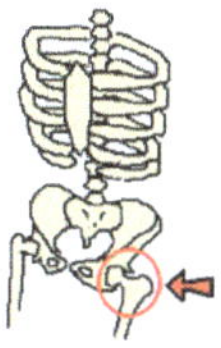   h ______

5 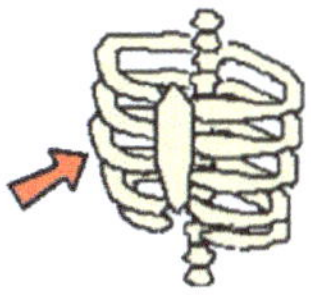   r ______

6 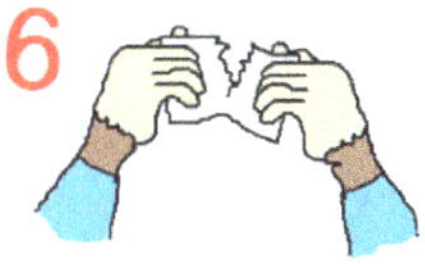   r ______

7 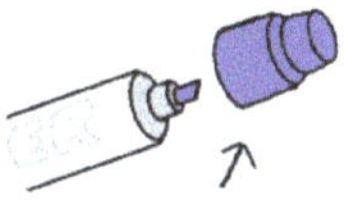   l ______

8 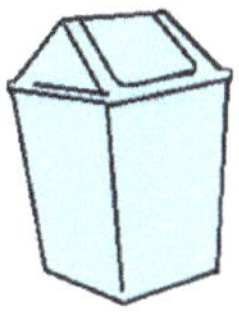   b ______

9 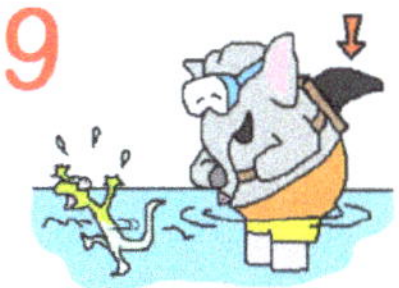   f ______

10 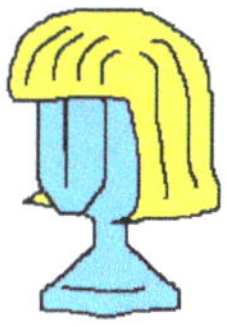   w ______

Listen and circle the right letters AND picture

1 ib ip in 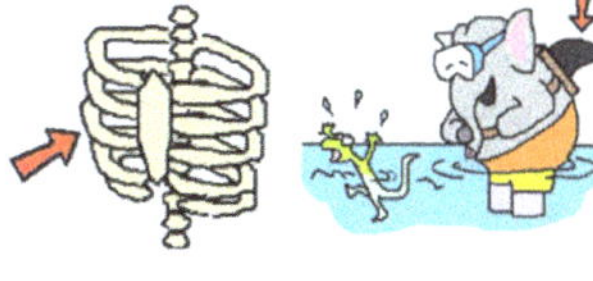

2 id in ib 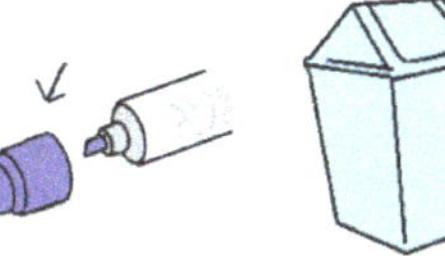

3 ip it ig 

4 id ib it 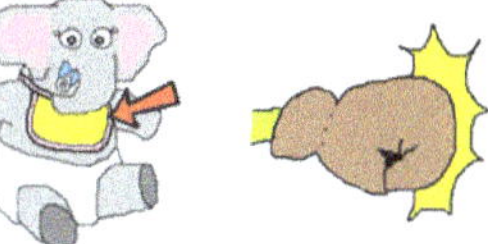

5 id ig it 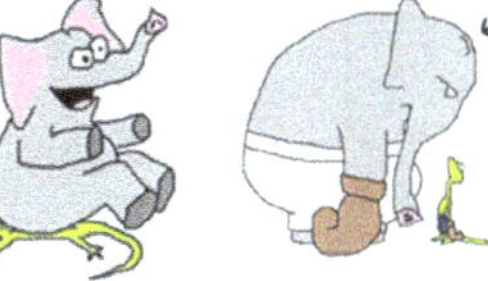

6 ip in ig 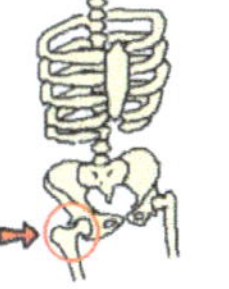

Exercises

Circle the word you hear

Write the word to match the picture

Chant

New sight words: want give me

Big kid sits in a bib.
Big kid sits in a bib.

I want ribs!
Give me ribs!

Big kid sits in a bib.

Story

Circle the last two letters of the word you hear

Tracks 30-39

1. ib ig ip   2. ib ig ip

3. it id in   4. it id in

5. in ig ib   6. in ig ip

Listen and read along

Sight words: him shut

Review

Listen and repeat all the words

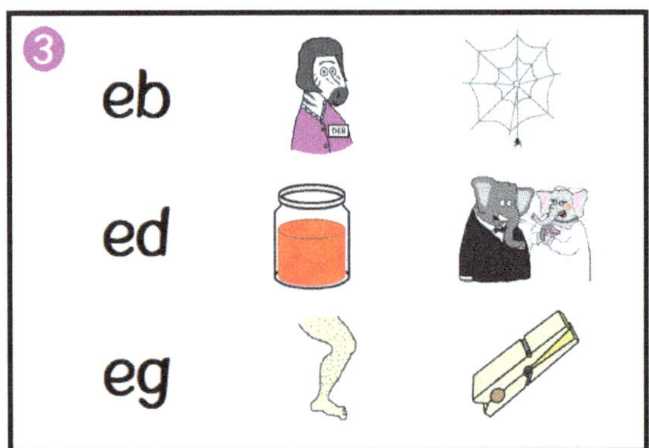

Review

1  ______________

2 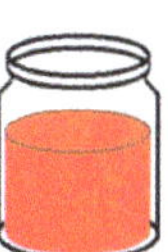 ______________

3  ______________

4  ______________

5  ______________

6 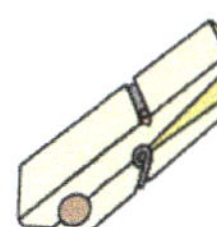 ______________

7  ______________

8  ______________

9  ______________

10  ______________

11  ______________

12  ______________

Review

Find the path

a        a

e   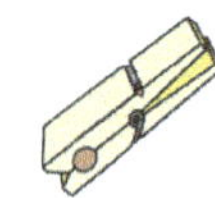   e

i 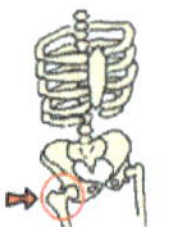     i

Listen to the final sound and circle the right one

Track 37

Tracks 30-39

1   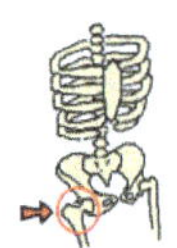 2  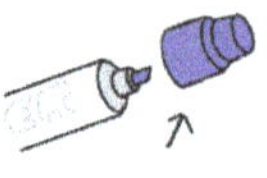 

3   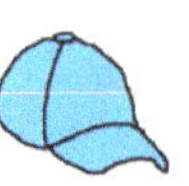 4  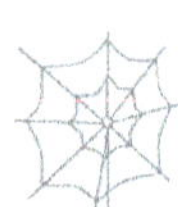 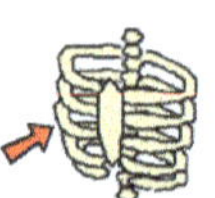

5    6  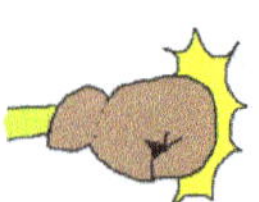 

7 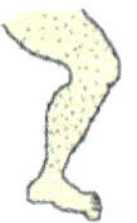   8   

Review

Listen and circle. Then write the word.

1

____

2

____

3
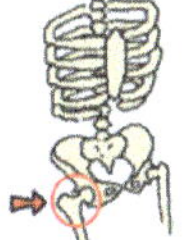
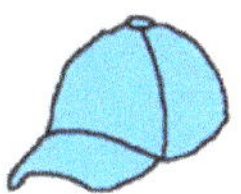

____

4

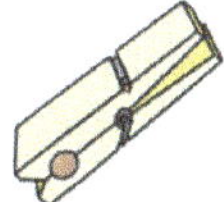
____

5

____

6

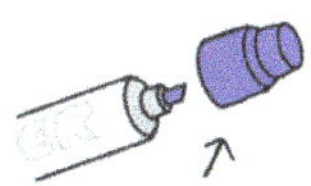
____

UNIT 4 — Short Vowel Sounds

Listen, point, and make the sound: Tracks 30-39 — Words with O 

1   o + b = ob 

2   o + t = ot 

3   o + x = ox 

Listen, point, and say the word: Track 40

1   r + ob = rob

2   p + ot = pot 

3   b + ox = box

Follow the rules

Write the words

1. **p** + **ot** = _______ 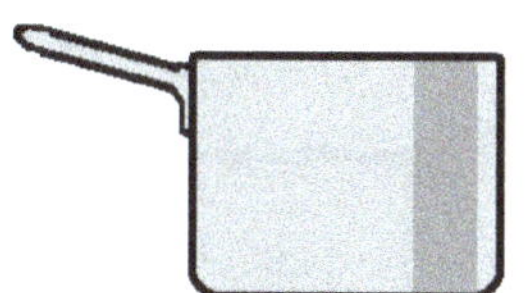

2. **r** + **ob** = _______ 

3. **b** + **ox** = _______ 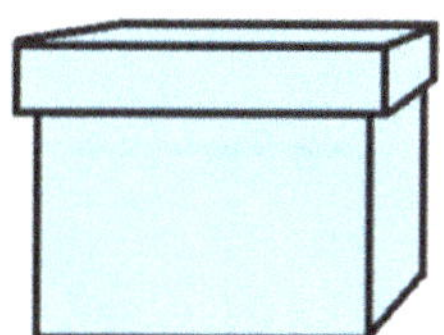

4. **R** + **on** = _______ 

5. **h** + **op** = _______ 

6. **d** + **og** = _______ 

New Words

Track 41

Tracks 40-49

ob

rob　　**sob**

og

dog　　**log**

on

on　　**Ron**

op

hop　　**mop**

ot

got　　**pot**

ox

box　　**fox**

Exercises

Listen and write the last two letters

1 l _______

2 s _______

3 d _______

4 h _______

5 _______

6 p _______

7 r _______

8 b _______

9 m _______

10 f _______

Listen and circle the right letters AND picture

1 ot ob on 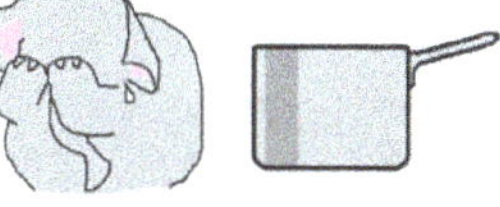

2 og op ox 

3 ob on ot 

4 ox og op 

5 on ot ob 

6 og op ox 

Exercises

Circle the word you hear

Tracks 40-49

Track 44

Write the word to match the picture

New sight words: he handsome pretty

Chant

Track 45

Dog on a log,
Dog on a log,
He's a handsome
Dog on a log.

Fox in a box,
Fox in a box,
She's a pretty
Fox in a box.

34   Unit 4

Story

Circle the last two letters of the word you hear

Track 46

Tracks 40-49

1 ot ob on   **2** ox og op

3 og op ox   **4** on ot ob

5 ob on ot   **6** og op ox

Listen and read along

Track 47

New words: Let's okay talk do or cent

UNIT 5   Short Vowel Sounds

Listen, point, and make the sound:   Track 48   Words with **u** 

Tracks 40-49

1   u + b = ub

2   u + n = un

3   u + t = ut

Listen, point, and say the word: Track 49 

1   t + ub = tub

2   f + un = fun

3   h + ut = hut

Follow the rules

1. t + ub = __________ 

2. f + un = __________ 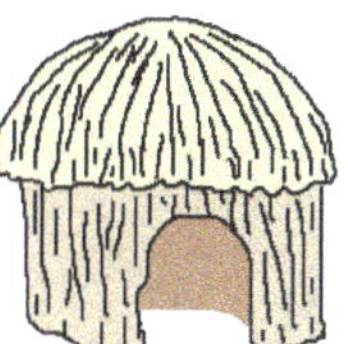

3. h + ut = __________ 

4. m + ud = __________ 

5. b + ug = __________ 

6. p + up = __________

New Words

Listen, point and repeat the new words

ub

sub   tub

ud

bud   mud

ug

bug   hug

un

fun   run

up

cup   pup

ut

cut   hut

Exercises

Listen and write the last two letters

1  t _______

2  b _______

3 s _______

4 h _______

5 r _______

6 p _______

7 h _______

8 f _______

9 c _______

10 m _______

Listen and circle the right letters AND picture

1 up ug un 

2 ub up ug 

3 ub un ud 

4 ub ug ut 

5 up ut ug 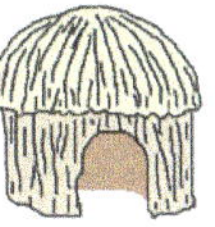 

6 ub ud un 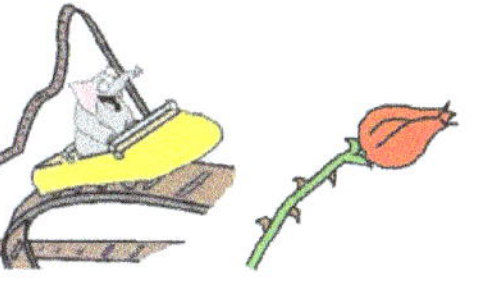

Exercises

Circle the word you hear

Tracks 50-59

Write the word to match the picture

Chant

Run pup,
Run pup run.
Run in the mud,
It's fun fun fun.

Run pup,
Run pup run.
Jump in the tub,
It's fun fun fun.

Story

Circle the last two letters of the word you hear

Track 55

Tracks 50-59

1. ut   un   up
2. ut   un   up
3. ud   ub   ug
4. ud   ut   ub
5. ug   ud   ub
6. ug   ud   up

Listen and read along  Track 56   Sight words: stop see too them many with

UNIT 6   Short Vowel Sounds

Listen, point, and make the sound:  Words with a,e,i,o,u

Tracks 50-59

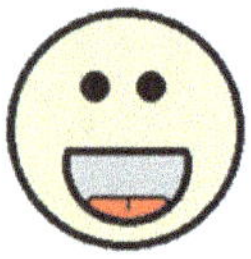

1 a + 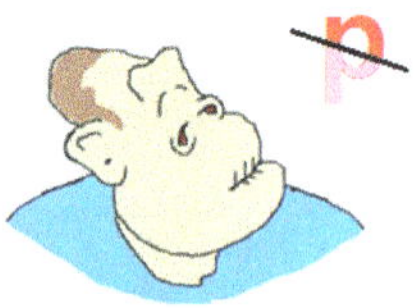 p = 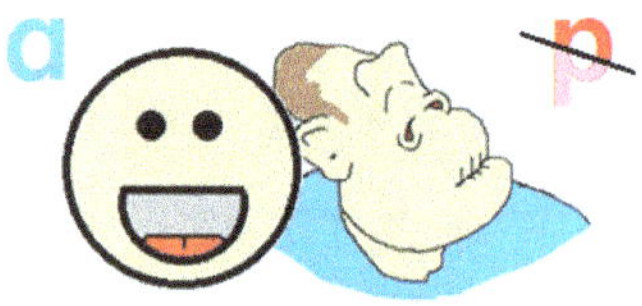 ap

Track 57

2 e + 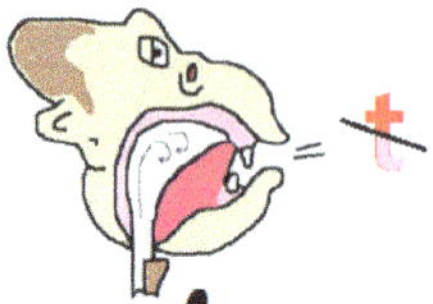 t = 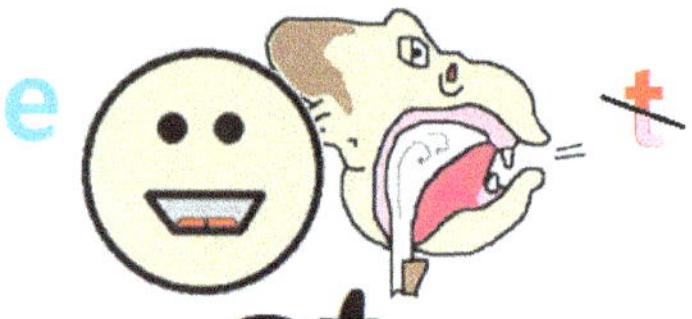 et

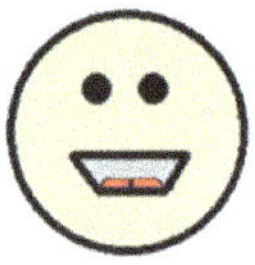

3 u + 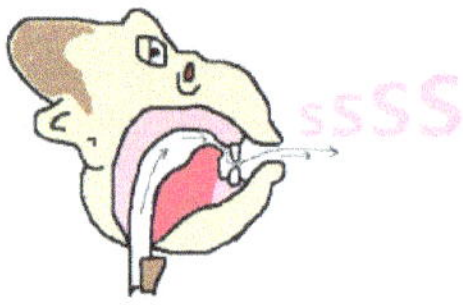 s = 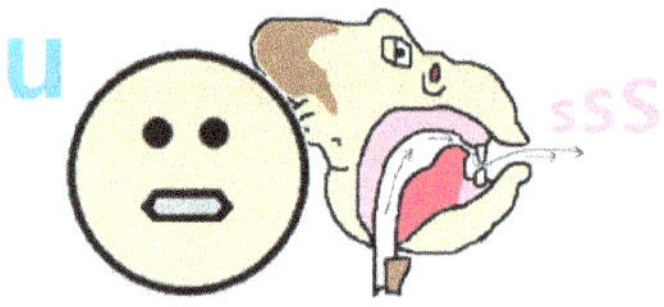 us

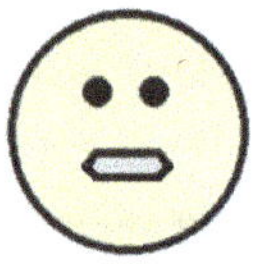

Listen, point, and say the word:  Track 58

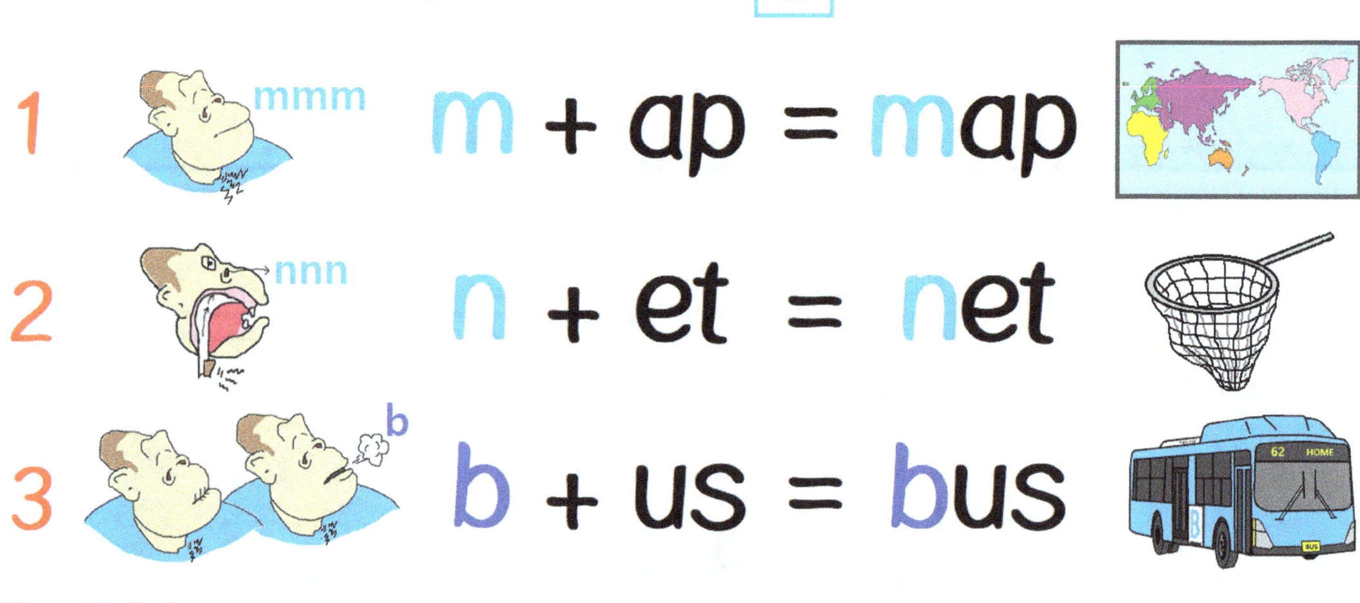

Write the words

1   **m** + **ap** = _________   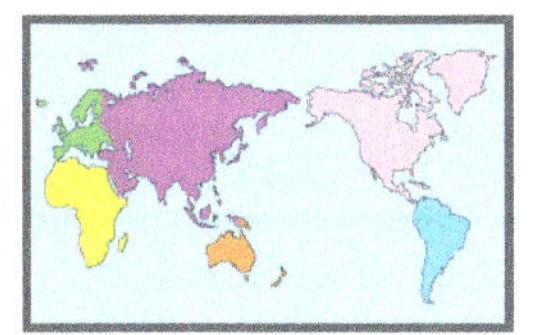

2   **n** + **et** = _________   

3   **b** + **us** = _________   

4   **c** + **op** = _________   

5   **p** + **ig** = _________   

6   **j** + **ug** = _________   

Tracks 50-59

Listen, point and repeat the new words

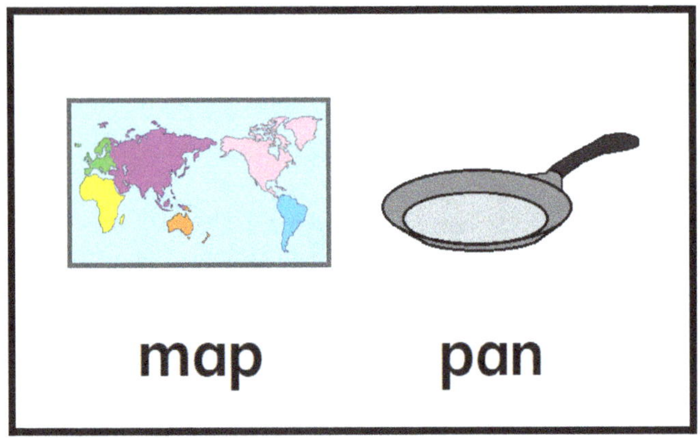

map   pan

bed   net

pig   win

cop   hot

bus   jug

Exercises

Listen and write the word

Tracks 60-69

1  _______________

2  _______________

3  _______________

4  _______________

5  _______________

6  _______________

7  _______________

8  _______________

9  _______________

10  _______________

Listen and circle the right letters AND picture

1 us ug at 

2 op et in 

3 ap un ig 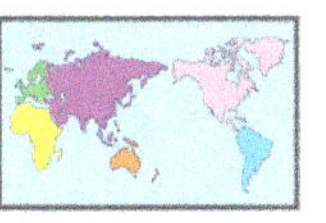

4 an et ad 

5 ap ig ed 

6 ot ag op 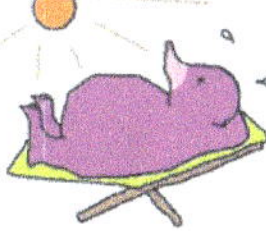

Exercises

Circle the word you hear

Write the word to match the picture

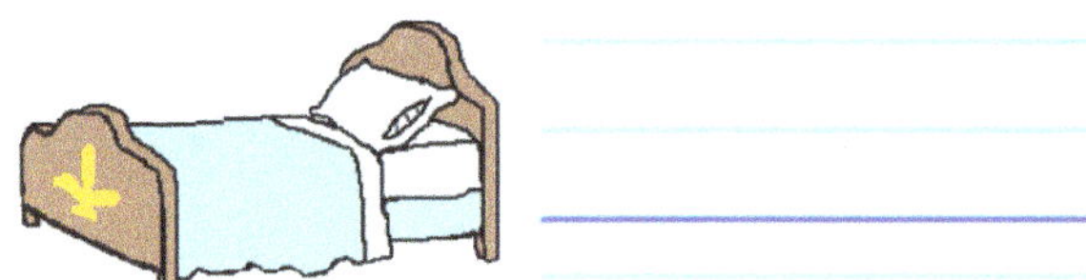

Chant

New sight words: call

Hot pig on a bus
Get the net

Hot pig on a bus
Get the net

Call a cop!
Call a cop!
Get the net

46   Unit 6

Story

Circle the last two letters of the word you hear

Track 64

Tracks 60-69

1. us   et   ug
2. ed   in   ap

3. et   ig   op
4. an   op   ug

5. ed   in   an
6. us   ap   ot

Listen and read along   Track 65

Sight words: must   now   need   maybe

Review

Track
66

Tracks 60-69

1
ob
og
on

2
op
ot
ox

3
ub
ud
ug

4
un
up
ut

5
ap
an
ed
et
ig

6
in
op
ot
us
ug

Review

Say the word and write it

1  __________

2  __________

3 __________

4  __________

5  __________

6  __________

7  __________

8  __________

9 __________

10 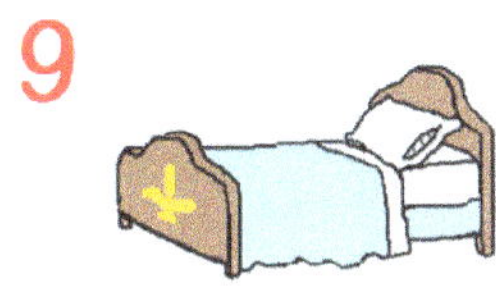 __________

11  __________

12  __________

Review

Find the path

a        a

e        e

i        i

o   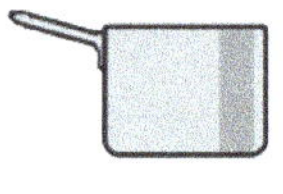  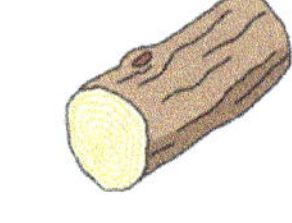   o

u  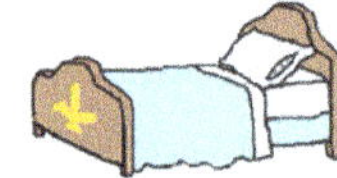  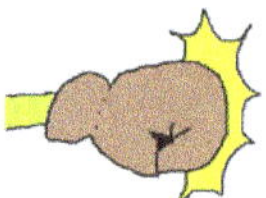    u

Listen to the final sound and circle the right word

1   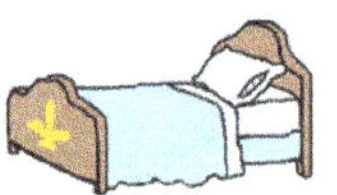   2   

3 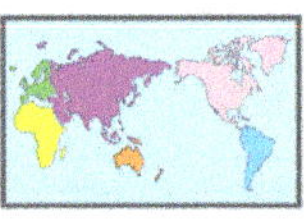     4   

5 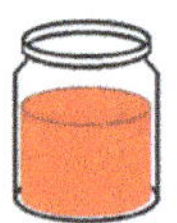 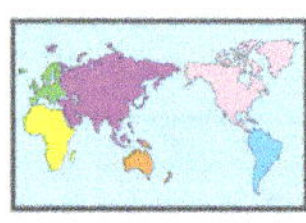 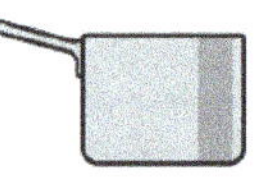   6   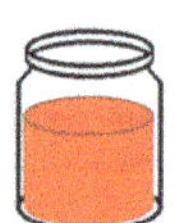

7  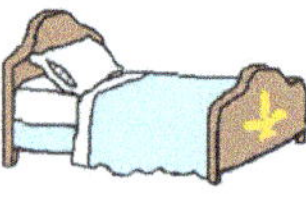    8    

Review

Listen and circle. Then write the word.

Tracks 60-69

1

2
    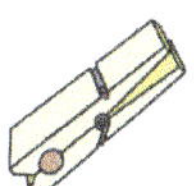

3
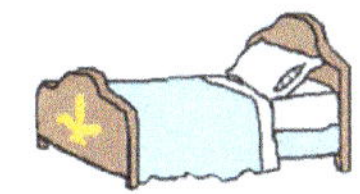    

4
   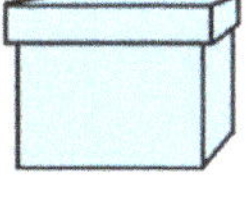 

5
 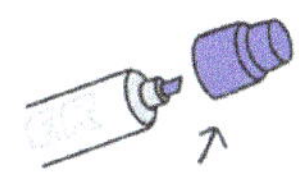   

6
   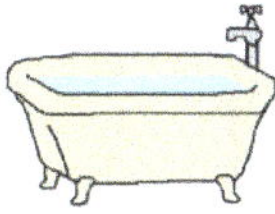 

Test

Listen and circle the word you hear

a 

b 

c 

Tracks 70-78

1       

2       

3       

4       

5  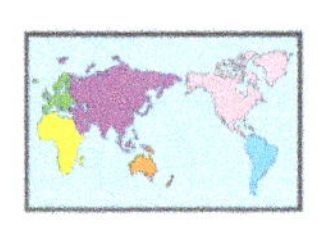  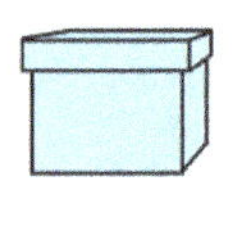   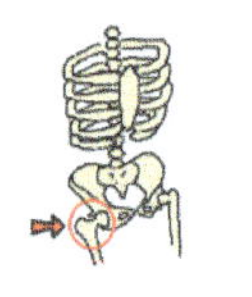

6   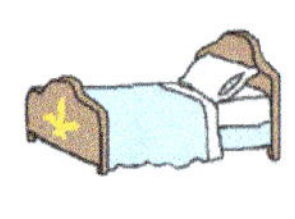    

7       

Test

Listen and write the middle letter

a  Track 72 b Track 73 c Track 74

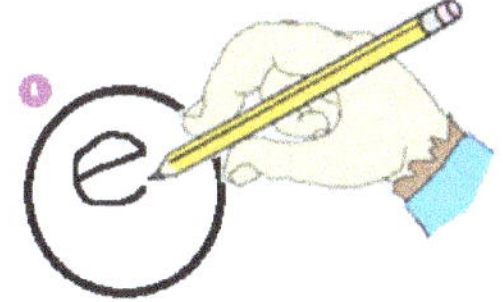

Tracks 70-77

1 2 3 4

5 6 7 8

9 10 11 12

13 14 15 16

Listen and circle the last two letters a  b  c 

Tracks 70-77

1  at | en | it | op | ut

2  ad | et | in | ob | un

3  ag | ed | id | og | up

4  an | eg | ip | ot | ub

5  am | ell | ib | on | ud

6  ap | eb | ig | ox | ug

Test

Write the word to match the picture

1 

2 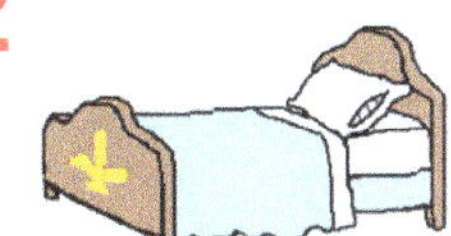

3 

4 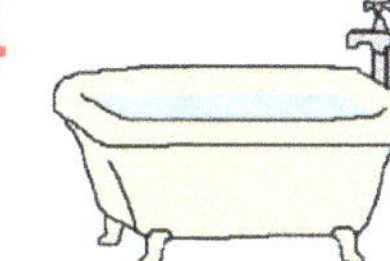

5 

6 

7 

8 

9 

10 

11 

12 

This is the end
of the book!

Word List

Unit 1

bad

dad

bag

nag

ham

jam

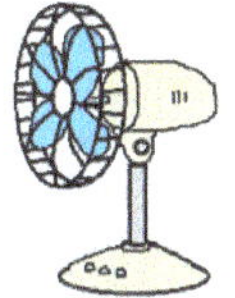

fan

man

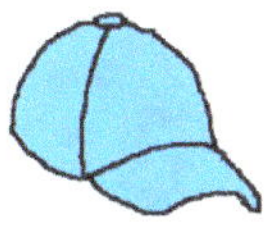

cap

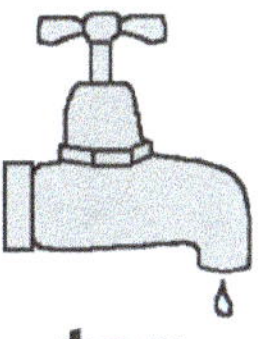

tap

fat

rat

Unit 2

Deb

web

red

wed

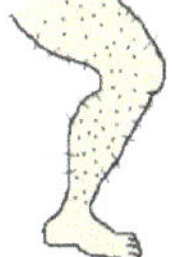

leg

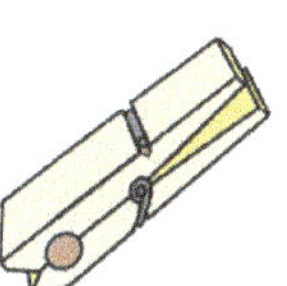

peg

bell

well

men

pen

pet

wet

Word List

Unit 3

bib

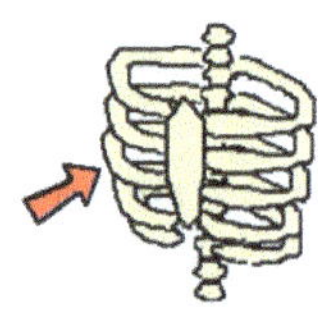

rib

kid

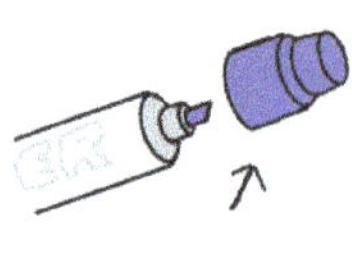

lid

big

wig

bin

fin

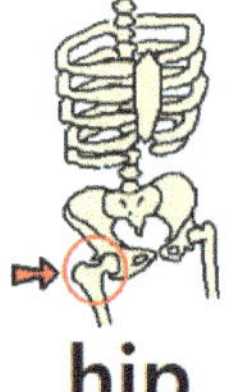

hip

rip

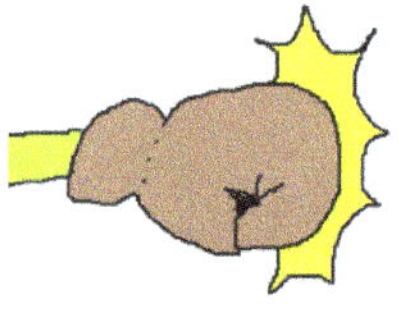

hit

sit

Unit 4

rob

sob

dog

log

on

Ron

hop

mop

got

pot

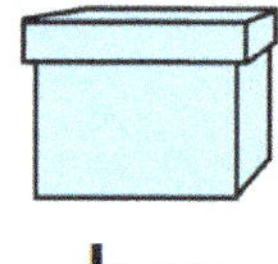

box

fox

Word List

Unit 5

sub

tub

bud

mud

bug

hug

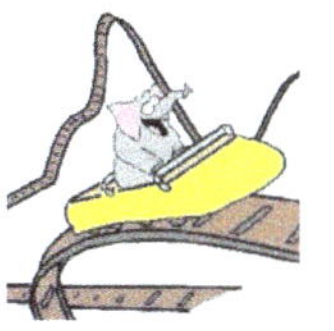
fun

run

cup

pup

cut

hut

Unit 6

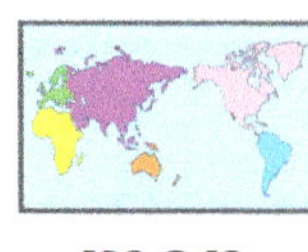
map

pan

bed

net

pig

win

cop

hot

bus

jug

Our Sight Words

Word	Note (ESL)	Word	Note (ESL)
a/an		by	
and		fellow	
all		say	
on		go	
in		to	
the		win	
no		I	
lift		had	
like		it	
get		wait	
oh		P13 have	
not		that	
did		yummy	
you		what	
your		P18 she	
yes		wear	
my		so	
has		scary	
put		will	
one		fell	

Our Sight Words

Word	Note (ESL)	Word	Note (ESL)
down		many	
am/are		with	
P24 want		P46 call	
give		must	
me		now	
him		need	
shut		maybe	
P34 he			
handsome			
pretty			
let's			
okay			
talk			
do			
or			
cent			
P41 stop			
see			
too			
them			

What's this page here for?

Well, those flashcards had to start on a odd page, and we had no content for this page.

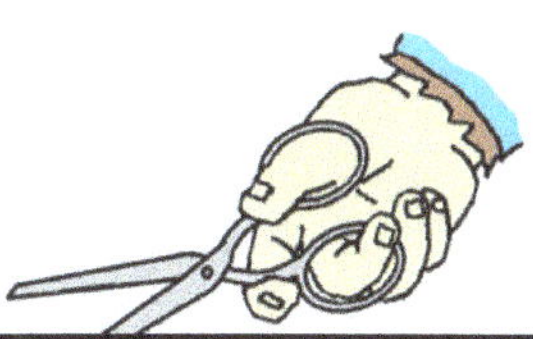

have	that
yummy	what
she	wear
so	scary

OUR SIGHT WORD FLASH CARDS!

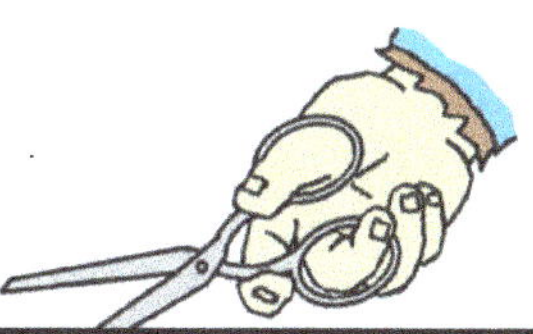

will	fell
down	am/are
want	give
me	him

OUR SIGHT WORD FLASH CARDS!

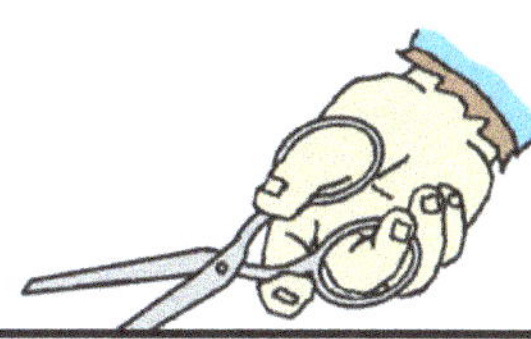

shut	he
handsome	pretty
let's	okay
talk	do

OUR SIGHT WORD FLASH CARDS!

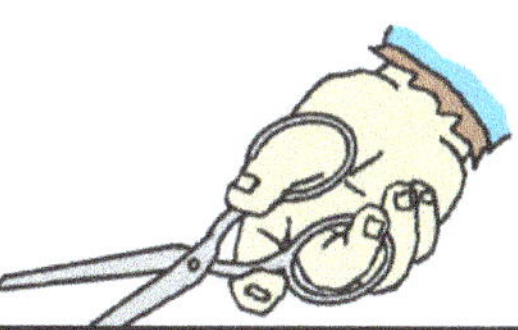

or

cent

stop

see

too

them

many

with

69

OUR SIGHT WORD FLASH CARDS!

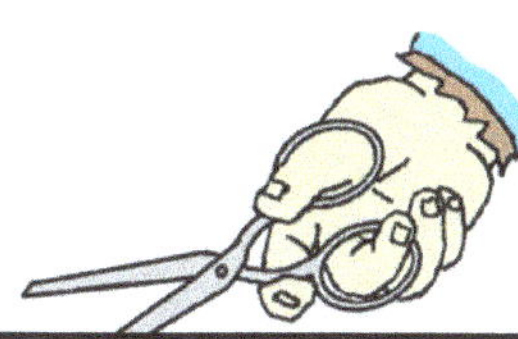

call	must
now	need
maybe	all
on	in

OUR SIGHT WORD FLASH CARDS!

the	no
lift	like
get	oh
not	did

OUR SIGHT WORD FLASH CARDS!

you	your
yes	my
has	put
one	by

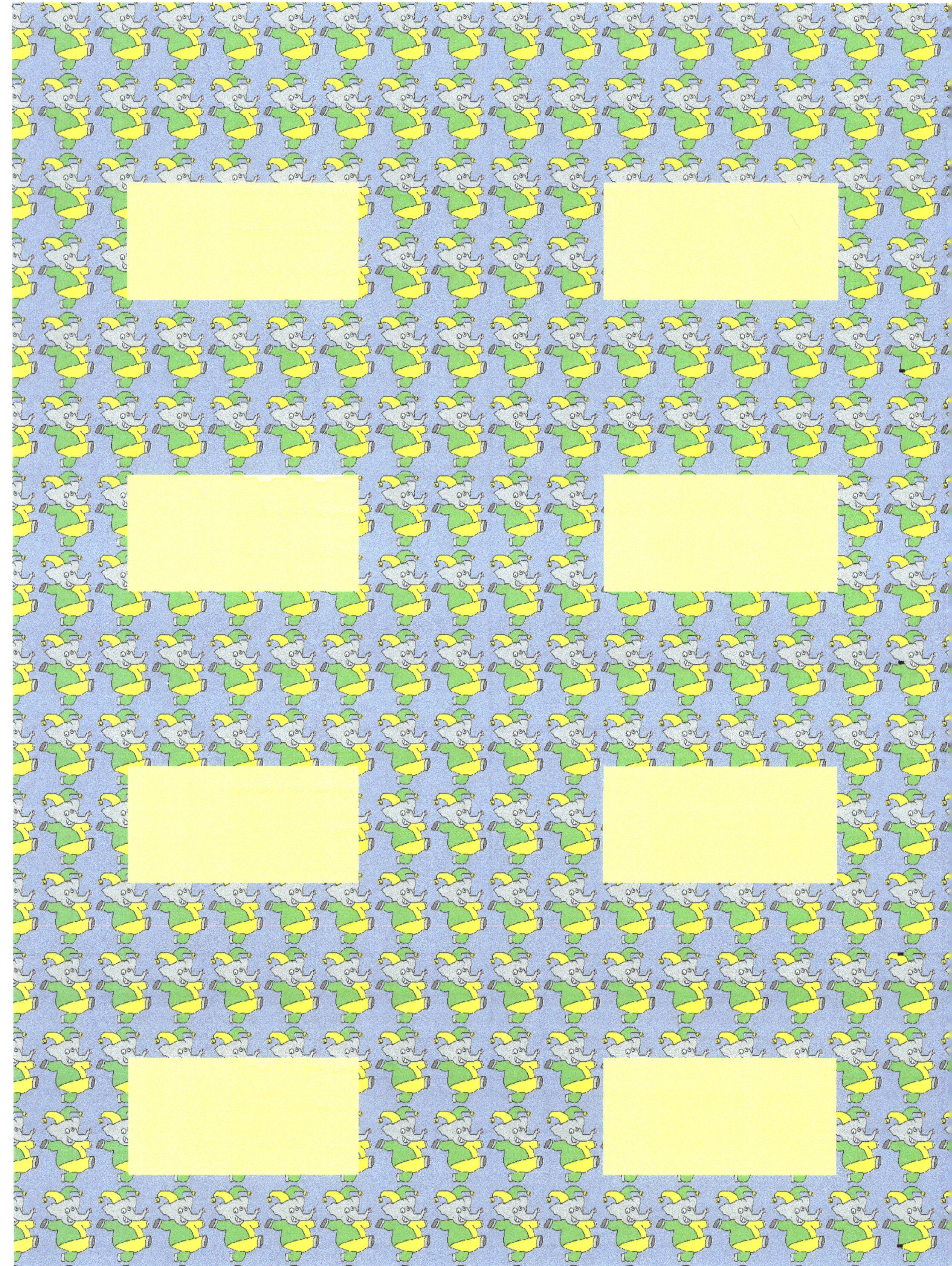

OUR SIGHT WORD FLASH CARDS!

say

go

to

win

had

it

wait

and

Phonics Series

Preschool:

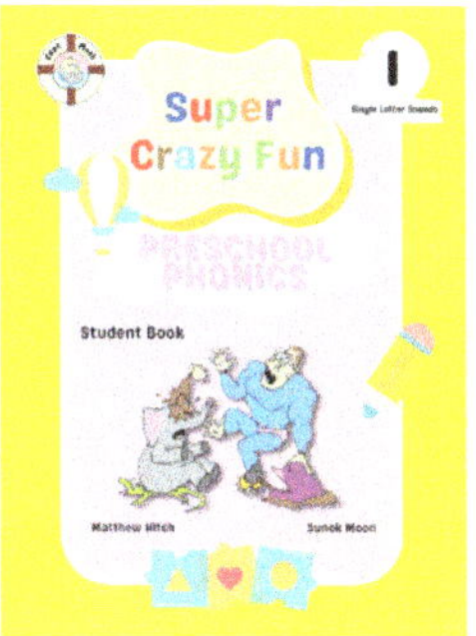    

Kindergarten:

   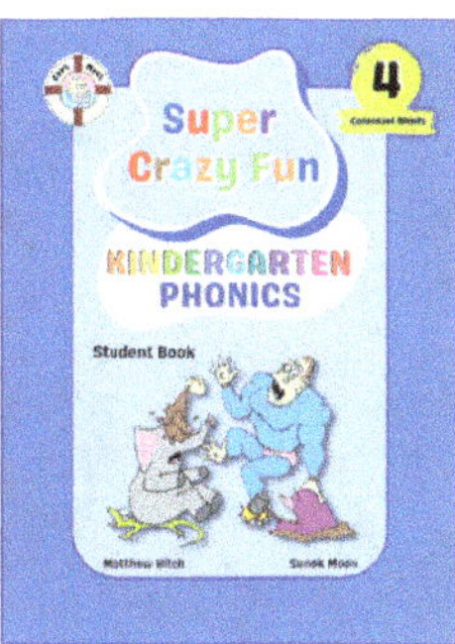 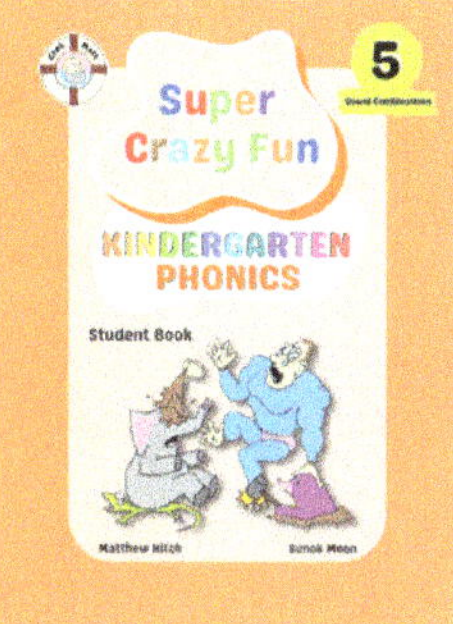

Elementary School Junior:

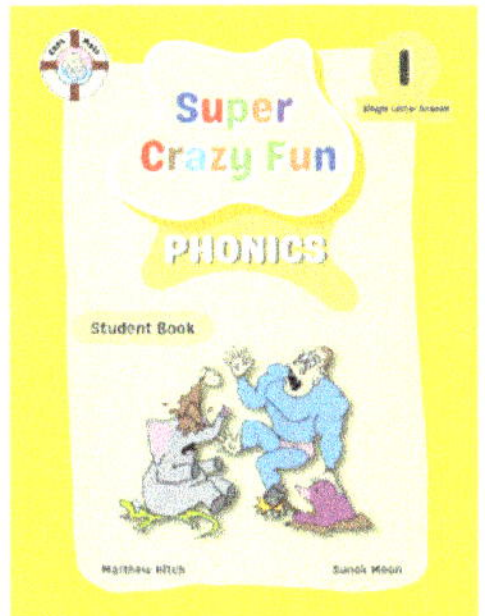 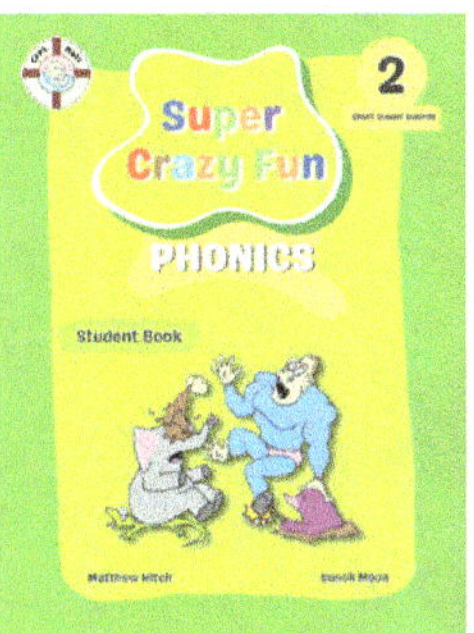 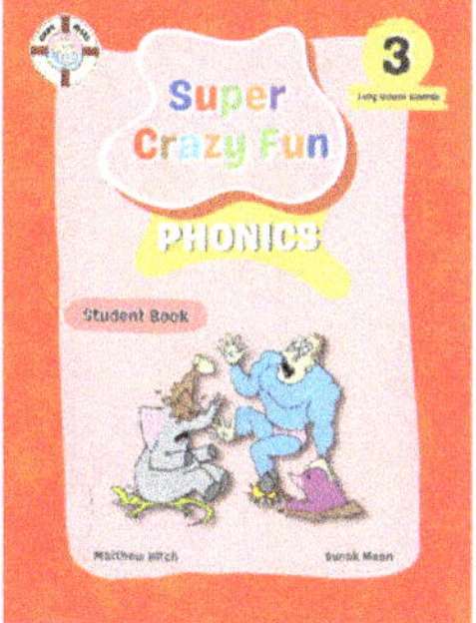  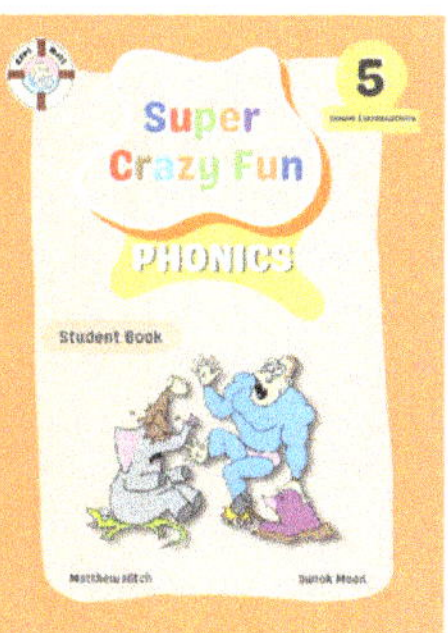

Elementary School Senior/Remedial:

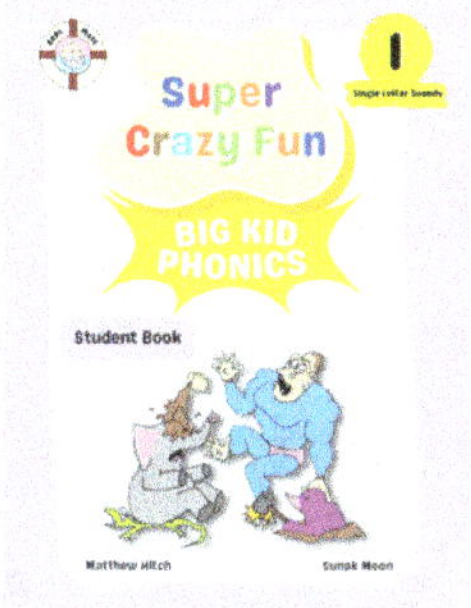  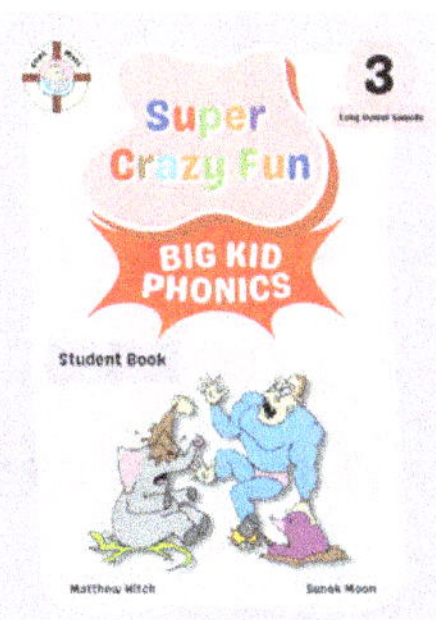 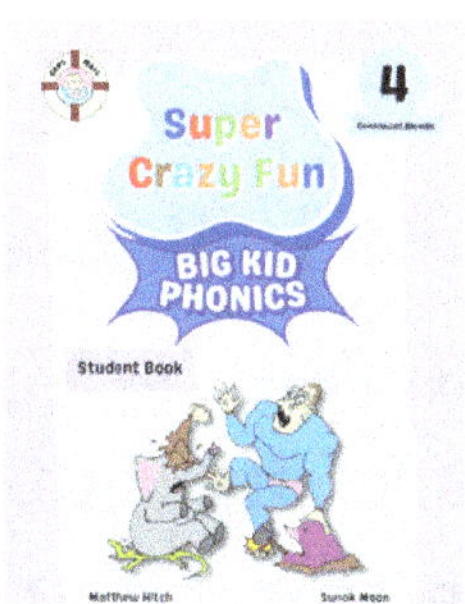 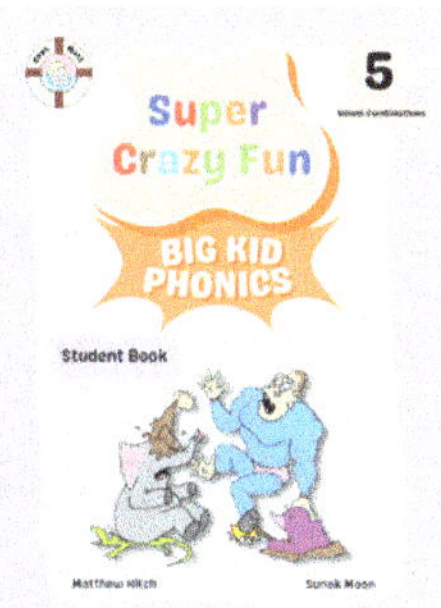

Incidentally, the contents of all these phonics books are available in one big silly book, too:

Have a look in Amazon or check our website: www.supercrazyfun.net (or just search online in case our publishing options have increased since this was printed.)

25	0	0	63	0	0	68	0	14	0	14	57	20	0	22	219
103	102	91	72	0	0	134	72	49	72	49	53	16	0	92	36
210	255	158	204	204	255	255	204	190	204	190	238	188	222	188	60

62	104	99	91	131	255	173	199	255	255	255	255	255	245	235	240
2	40	31	6	68	0	68	69	128	0	128	108	83	114	95	117
202	253	226	176	176	255	200	196	255	255	192	156	169	153	175	197

255	255	222	237	219	238	242	237	254	255	243	252	255	253	255	244
0	0	33	18	36	32	60	81	96	115	125	149	145	181	255	225
0	19	52	95	60	94	6	35	1	0	29	46	77	83	123	89

251	240	255	255	239	228	194	151	53	90	20	3	3	66	12	27
238	228	255	247	250	241	235	228	217	186	224	241	134	99	81	82
0 *	11	0	91	44	65	71	35	102	74	158	211	190	191	243	226